Mystifying MATH PUZZLES

Steve Ryan

STERLING PUBLISHING CO., INC.
NEW YORK

Contents

Edited by Claire Bazinet

10   9   8   7   6   5   4   3   2

Published in 1996 by Sterling Publishing Company, Inc.
387 Park Avenue South, New York, N.Y. 10016
© 1996 by Steve Ryan
Distributed in Canada by Sterling Publishing
℅ Canadian Manda Group, One Atlantic Avenue, Suite 105
Toronto, Ontario, Canada M6K 3E7
Distributed in Great Britain and Europe by Cassell PLC
Wellington House, 125 Strand, London WC2R 0BB, England
Distributed in Australia by Capricorn Link (Australia) Pty Ltd.
P.O. Box 6651, Baulkham Hills, Business Centre, NSW 2153, Australia
Manufactured in the United States of America
All rights reserved

Sterling ISBN 0-8069-1304-5

A Note to the Reader

In your quest for number nirvana you've discovered the quintessential mother lode of numerical shenanigans. Ever notice that when you've misplaced or lost something you always find it in the last place you look (think about it)? Well, this book is filled with lost, hidden, and missing number puzzles all designed to have you searching the nooks, crannies, and outer limits of your imagination.

So, put on your thinking caps and prepare to explore a nebula of number puzzles, posers, and pastimes. It's time to test your number I.Q. Before you is a competitive arena for the mind in which you will enjoy the rewards of great self-satisfaction. Some puzzles ask you to apply the basics: addition, subtraction, multiplication and division; while others require more abstract calculations and number navigations. There are magic squares, mathematical mazes, devious dissections, logic problems of weights and dates, coin and matchstick maneuvers, and even word games all based on numerical knowledge.

Puzzles throughout the book vary in degree of complexity. At a puzzle's first glance you might experience "Total Confusion" (page 13), but with a little "Yankee Ingenuity" (page 39) each of these number-crunching conundrums poses a fair challenge and requires no formal mathematical training. The difficulty of each puzzle is rated as a one, two, or three penciller. Although the one-pencil puzzlers are the easiest, they still require considerable flexing of your mental muscles. Three-pencil puzzlers are the toughest nuts to crack: these gruelers demand rigorous cerebral calisthenics to decipher or divine.

If you're up to the challenge, and I'm sure you are, you're in for a terrific think test and googols of fun. For, whether you're a "Mathemagician" or a "Number Novice," all of these puzzles are guaranteed to intrigue.

So sharpen your pencils, and sharpen your wits. You may be a lot more numberwise than you think!

Steve Ryan

1
The World's Easiest Maze

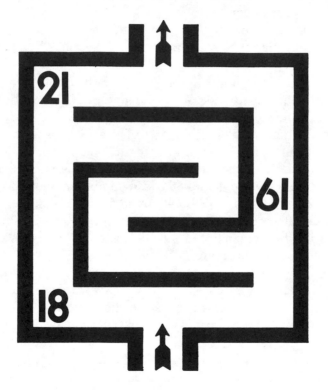

Travel through this maze totaling exactly 100 points. No passage or intersection may be used more than once. Enter and exit the maze at the designated arrows.

Solution on page 82.

WATTS WRONG?

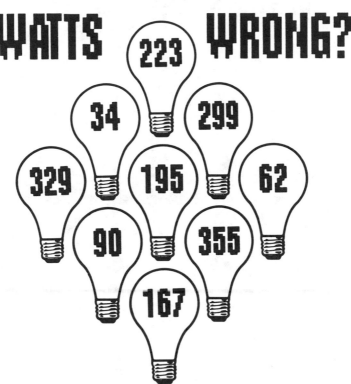

Three light bulbs in this puzzle have been incorrectly numbered by plus or minus one. It is your challenge to determine which bulbs need to be changed and correct their numbers to create a magic square in which the horizontal row, vertical row, and all six diagonal rows of three bulbs total the same number.

Solution on page 84.

(Need a clue? Turn to page 8.)

POSITIVE PLACEMENT

The nine numbered blocks in this puzzle predetermine the numeric value of all twenty-seven remaining blocks. Solve as follows: 1) Each subdivision of four blocks must reveal the numbers one, two, three, and four. 2) Adjacent blocks (horizontally or vertically) may never be of identical numeric value, even if they are in different subdivisions.

Solution on page 86.

4

OAKIE DOKIE

The age of three grand oaks totals exactly one thousand years. From the following information, determine the age of each tree: When the youngest tree has reached the age of the middle tree, the middle tree will be the age of the oldest tree and four times the current age of the youngest tree.

Solution on page 88.

5

FLOATING HEDGES #1

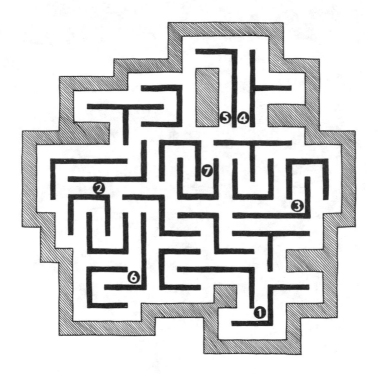

Draw a continuous line through this maze, connecting the numbers one through seven consecutively. You may not travel the same passageway more than once.

Solution on page 90.

Clue to puzzle **2**: *Each row totals 585.*

FOUR WARNED

Things are not always what they appear to be. This may be the easiest dissection puzzle you'll ever tackle. It all depends on how you approach the problem. Two fathers and two sons wish to divide this irregular-shaped parcel of land evenly among themselves. Each parcel must be identical in size and shape. How can this be done?

Solution on page 92.

BROKEN PENTAGRAM

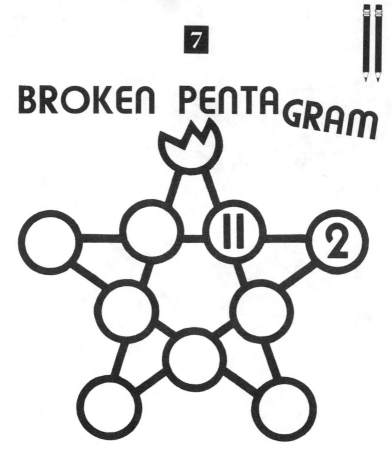

It's possible to position ten consecutive numbers on an unbroken pentagram of ten circles in such a way that each straight line of four circles totals exactly the same number. Here we issue the same challenge but with a little twist. Of ten consecutive numbers place nine in the nine unbroken circles in such a way that each straight line of three or four unbroken circles totals exactly twenty-four. Two numbers have been positioned for you.

Solution on page 94.

(Need a clue? Turn to page 12.)

8

SQUARE SHOOTER

A standard checkerboard measures 8 squares by 8 squares and contains 32 black squares and 32 red squares. Exactly 139 other size checkerboards, ranging from 2 by 2 to 7 by 7 squares, exist on a standard checkerboard. How many of these smaller-size checkerboards can be found, that also contain an equal number of red and black squares.

Solution on page 82.

PRIME BEEF

Here's a magic-square puzzle in which the un-branded eight heads of beef must be branded with a prime number (numbers that can only be divided evenly by one and itself) in such a way that each horizontal, vertical, and diagonal row of three cows totals 111. The lowest and only non-prime number brand ("1": an even more elite digit) in the puzzle has been placed to give you a head start.

Solution on page 84.

Clue to puzzle **7**: *Throw out the number five.*

TOTAL CONFUSION

Travel from "A" to "B" scoring the lowest possible score. The passages comprising the puzzle cross over and under one another and only intersect at the circles.

Solution on page 86.

(Need a clue? Turn to page 15.)

LOVE BUGS

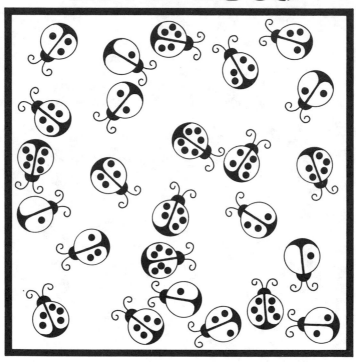

All of the love bugs in this puzzle are sporting from one to six spots on their backs. Your task is to mate six pairs of these love bugs by drawing straight lines that connect two bugs sporting the same number of spots. Further, the six pairs to be mated must include love bugs from each spotted denomination (one through six). At no time may lines or bugs be crossed over in solving this puzzle.

Solution on page 88.

five card draw

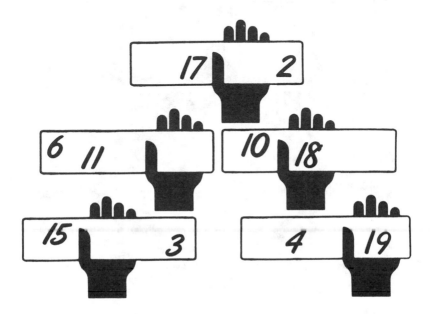

To solve this puzzle, place two additional numbers on each of the five cards. The final solution must reveal the numbers one through twenty and each card must total the same number.

Solution on page 90.

(Need a clue? turn to page 19.)

Clue to puzzle **10**: *Seven is the lowest possible score.*

SQUARE DEAL

Take the numbers two through nine and square them (2 × 2, 3 × 3, etc.). Now place each of these squared numbers in the nine vacant squares so that each row of four squares totals 102. One squared number (1 × 1), which appears four times, has already been positioned.

Solution on page 92.

ZER**O** HOUR

Travel through this maze connecting each of the six spots with one continuous meandering line. No passageway or intersection may be used more than once. Your starting and finishing points are located in the dead-end passages.

Solution on page 94.

ROUND TRIPPER

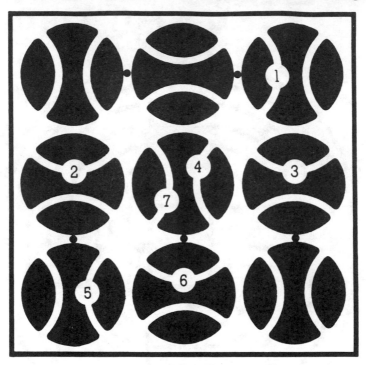

For this nine-ball maze, connect the numbers one through seven consecutively with one single continuous line and then return back to one. Throughout your journey you must pass through all eighteen ball seams exactly once. Further ground rules restrict normal passage between adjacent balls or walls next to balls to only once, and five dots positioned between balls block passage completely.

Solution on page 82.

MATCH WITS #1

Here's a two-part matchstick puzzle designed to prove that half of eleven is six. First, rearrange two matches to reveal the number eleven. Then remove half of the matches to reveal the number six.

Solution on page 88.

Clue to puzzle **12**: *Each card must total forty-two.*

house call

Pick any house as your starting point and trace a route in the following manner that visits all twenty-four of the remaining houses without ever revisiting a single house: Follow one wire to the first house, follow two wires to the second house, follow three wires to the third house and repeat this pattern over and over until all twenty-four houses are visited.

Solution on page 86.

(Need a clue? Turn to page 23.)

THE PERFECT PYRAMID

?
28
496
8,128
130,816
2,096,128

What is the missing number that belongs on top of this pyramid and begins this progressively growing logical number sequence?

Solution on page 84.

NINE GOOD YEARS

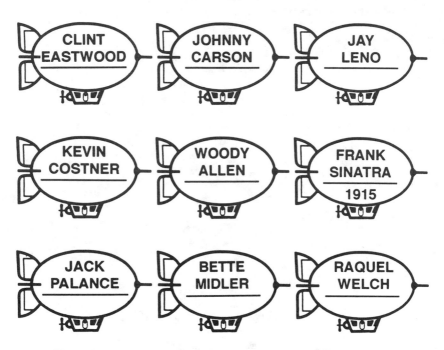

Hovering in nine blimps are nine talented superstars. They were born in the years 1915, 1920, 1925, 1930, 1935, 1940, 1945, 1950, and 1955. Correctly date each celebrity with the appropriate year of birth (as illustrated by Sinatra's airship) and you'll create a magic square in which each horizontal, vertical, and diagonal row of three blimps totals the same number. A couple of educated guesses should get you airborne.

Solution on page 90.

(Need a clue? Turn to page 25.)

BOB ON WEAVE

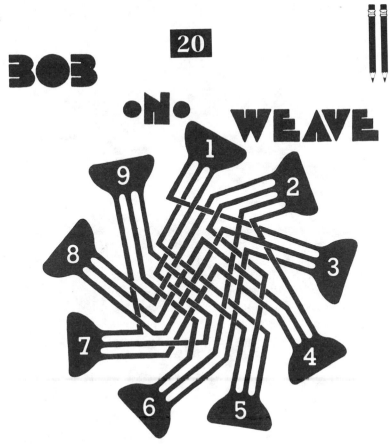

This numerical maze consists of nine numbered stations connected by fourteen crisscrossing pathways that only intersect at stations. Your task is to find a route that starts and finishes at station one and visits each of the remaining stations exactly once. At no time may any pathway be utilized more than once.

This puzzle has two possible solutions. Can you find both?

Solution on page 92.

Clue to puzzle **17**: *Finish at the center house.*

Key Decision #1

The numbered keys above correspond to the locked corridors in the puzzle. It is your challenge to select only three keys that will unlock the correct corridors and allow passage from one sunburst room to the other.

Solution on page 94.

22

HOUSE OF DOTS

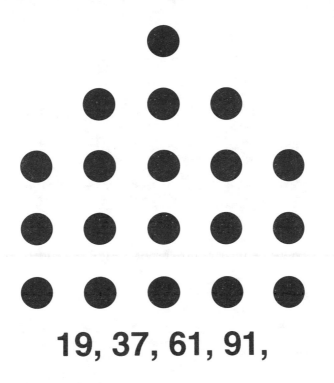

19, 37, 61, 91,

Your challenge in this puzzle is to find the next number in the mathematical sequence above. Carefully study the illustrated house of dots for it provides the key to the secret of the sequence.

Solution on page 82.

Clues to puzzle **19**: *Each row totals 5805, Kevin Costner is the youngest.*

25

IT'S GREEK TO ME

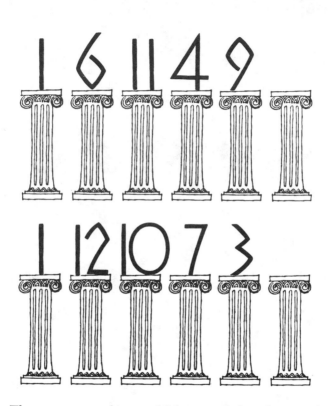

These two puzzles would have perplexed even the cleverest of ancient Greeks. Time will tell if you're clever enough to position a number atop each of the vacant columns to complete these two separate numerical-sequence problems.

Solution on page 84.

(Need a clue? Turn to page 28.)

Matching 4sum

$$
\begin{array}{r}
Q\,Q \\
Q.Q \\
\hline
?
\end{array}
$$

Illustrated above are two math problems in one. For one, you must add the numbers together. In the other, you must multiply them. Both problems must produce the identical sum and product. It is your task to determine the numerical value of "Q" and reveal the identical answers.

Solution on page 86.

THE $10,000 PYRAMID

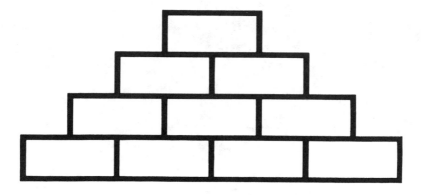

Using only the number four, place ten money amounts in the ten blocks of this pyramid to total $10,000.

Solution on page 88.

Clue to puzzle **23**: *Big Ben could help you solve these puzzles.*

26

SITTING DUCKS

There are three different kinds of ducks in this puzzle. Position six more ducks on this two-dimensional pond so that each of the five horizontal and vertical rows will sport all three different kinds of sitting ducks.

Solution on page 90.

CASE CLOSED

Before you are nine cases labeled with the letters "E", "F", "S" or "T". It is known that inside each case is a different number that begins with the letter seen on the outside of the case. Example: "T" could stand for two, three, ten, and so on. It is your challenge to determine all nine numbers to reveal a magic square in which each horizontal, vertical, and diagonal row of three cases totals exactly the same.

Solution on page 94.

(Need a clue? Turn to page 34.)

OPTICAL DIVERSION

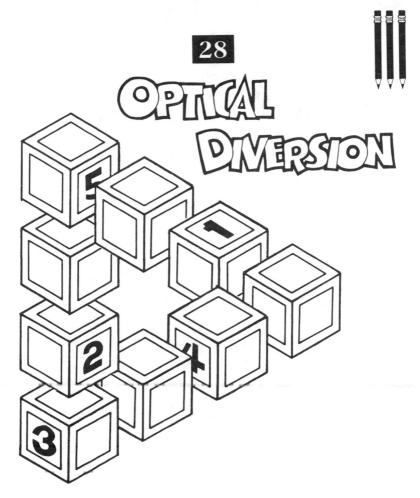

Using the numbers one through nine three times each, number the remaining surfaces of the cubes in such a way that each cube totals exactly fifteen. In doing so, you must also assure that each row of four cube surfaces in a straight row and facing the same direction (up, left, or right) must total twenty. Example: The two cube surfaces three and four above are in a straight line, facing left. There are nine such rows to be completed.

Solution on page 92.

31

PHONY NUMBERS #1

Here is a coded word game in which the telephone is instrumental in converting numbers to letters. As seen on a touch-tone or dial phone, each of the numbers used in this puzzle can represent one of three different letters. It is your challenge to convert each line of numbers into a word which is related to its puzzle category. It takes one smooth operator to answer the call for each line of phony numbers in this collection of three categories.

Solution on page 82.

CHILDHOOD GAMES

A•467726824
B•52257
C•6272537
D•53273764
E•824

THINGS YOU OBSERVE

A•7222284
B•5297
C•46543297
D•78277
E•2878667

ON AN AIRPLANE

A•2244243
B•66843
C•74568
D•7839273377
E•327746637

30

BURNING BRIDGES

Think of each match in this puzzle as a bridge that must be supported by two coins, one at each end. Your challenge is to arrange the four nickels, one dime, and seven matches to fulfill the following requirements: 1) Five matches must be supported by ten cents. 2) Two matches must be supported by fifteen cents. 3) No two matches may be supported by the same two coins.

Solution on page 86.

Clues to puzzle **27** : *Each row totals 36, the smallest number used is four.*

HOLLYWOOD SQUARES

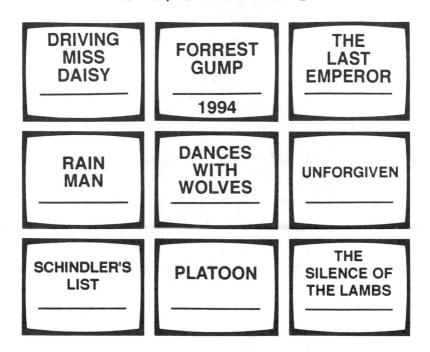

DRIVING MISS DAISY ____	**FORREST GUMP** ____ **1994**	**THE LAST EMPEROR** ____
RAIN MAN ____	**DANCES WITH WOLVES**	**UNFORGIVEN** ____
SCHINDLER'S LIST ____	**PLATOON** ____	**THE SILENCE OF THE LAMBS** ____

Supply the correct year that each of these Academy Award–winning movies won their Oscars for Best Motion Picture and you'll create a magic square in which each horizontal, vertical, and diagonal row of three screens totals the same number. To get you started, it is given that *Forrest Gump* won in 1994.

Solution on page 84.

(Need a clue? Turn to page 39.)

RERACKUM

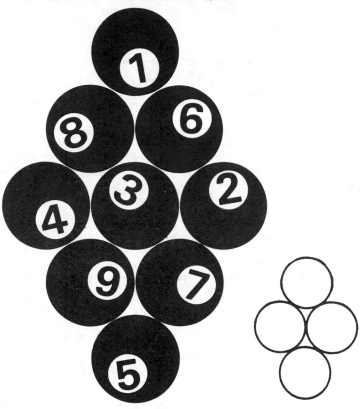

This vertical diamond of nine billiard balls contains four smaller vertical diamonds of four balls (as seen in the sample above) which overlap and share various balls with other diamonds in the rack. It is your challenge to switch the fewest number of balls to assure that each of the four diamonds totals exactly the same number.

Solution on page 88.

Cross Examination #1

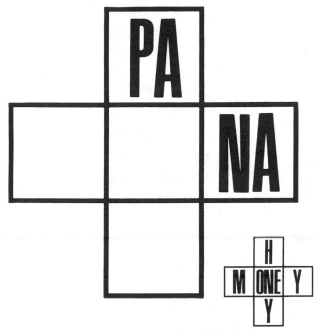

In the small sample puzzle illustrated, four letters (H, M, Y, Y) and one number (one) fill the five squares to create a mini-crossword number puzzle that spells "money" across and "honey" down. Your task is to solve the partially completed puzzle above by positioning one number in the center square and a total of four letters in the remaining two squares to reveal two words that fit the following clues:

Across: A "touching" feature
Down: Government numbers

Solution on page 90.

DIVIDE AND CONJURE

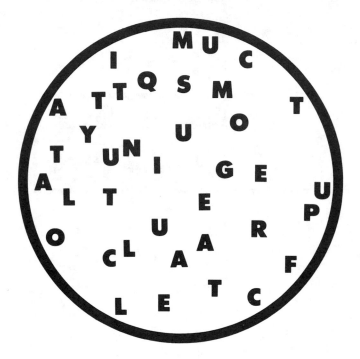

Use three straight lines to divide this circular playing field into six sections. If the lines are drawn correctly, the letters within each section can be unscrambled to reveal six related words, all associated with counting.

Solution on page 92.

(Need a clue? Turn to page 41.)

PENNY WISE

The centers of four pennies are positioned at the corners of the illustrated square. It is your task to reposition two pennies to create a new square exactly half the size of the existing square.

Solution on page 94.

Clues to puzzle **31**: Each row of three screens totals 5970. The oldest film won in 1987.

Head Start

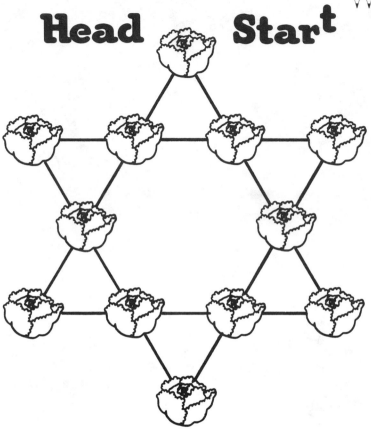

These twelve heads of lettuce are planted in such a way as to create six straight rows each containing four heads of lettuce. Can you plant a garden using another configuration which fulfills these same requirements?

Solution on page 83.

(Need a clue? Turn to page 44.)

FLOATING HEDGES #2

Draw a continuous line through this maze which connects the numbers one through eight consecutively. You may never travel the same passageway more than once.

Solution on page 85.

Clue to puzzle **34** : *Two of the unscrambled words are "quantity" and "figure."*

Travel through this maze scoring the highest possible number of points. Begin by selecting a number of your choice. Your journey must begin and end at this number. Throughout your journey your path must always flow with the arches. Example: From "1" you may only travel to "3" or "4". At no time may you retravel any passage. Top score is 66 if you can visit all eleven numbers.

Solution on page 86.

(Need a clue? Turn to page 47.)

Six great Yankee ballplayers (Yogi Berra, Clete Boyer, Joe DiMaggio, Lou Gehrig, Mickey Mantle, and Babe Ruth) are each positioned on two base paths of this triple-decker infield. These players are most famous for wearing the numbers three, four, five, six, seven, and eight. Your challenge is to correctly match each uniform number with the correct Yankee to insure that each of the three different base paths will total exactly twenty-two.

Solution on page 88.

(Need a clue? Turn to page 49.)

Round Numbers #1

Position one letter in each of the five between-spoke openings on this wagon wheel. Do this in such a manner that three numbers are spelled out that total thirteen. Words may be written clockwise and counterclockwise and, as in traditional crossword puzzles, individual letters may be shared. Example: On a larger wheel, four and five could be written: R-U-O-F-I-V-E.

Solution on page 90.

(Need a clue? Turn to page 52.)

Clue to puzzle **36**: *Begin with a square four-by-four grid. Then eliminate four lettuce heads.*

MAGIC WORD SQUARES

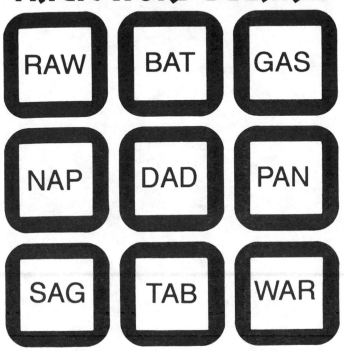

Each letter in this puzzle represents a different number from zero to nine. It is your challenge to switch these letters back to numbers in such a way that each horizontal, vertical, and diagonal row of three words totals the same number. Your total for this puzzle is 1515. It is known that "tab" is the highest scoring word and "raw" is the second highest scoring word.

Solution on page 92.

(Need a clue? Turn to page 53.)

ARROWHEADINGS

In this maze, your course headings are predetermined and point values have been assigned to each passage. Starting from the bottom intersection, travel to each of the other five intersections and return to the beginning intersection with the lowest possible point score.

Solution on page 94.

(Need a clue? Turn to page 55.)

Wicked Number

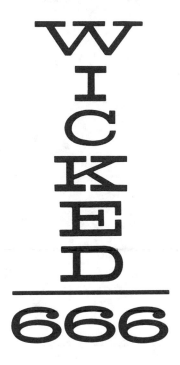

At present this puzzle really only totals 601. That's because three of the letters in "wicked" do not belong. You must eliminate the bogus letters and substitute the correct three letters to achieve the desired total.

Solution on page 83.

Clue to puzzle 38 : Begin at number six.

44

EQUATOR XING

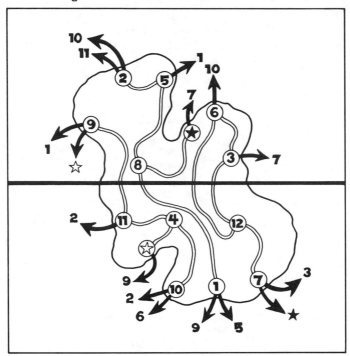

There are twelve numerical destinations (1 through 12) on this tiny tropical island. You must start your journey at one of the two stars and then travel to each number on the map and ultimately finish at the other star. At no time may any number be visited more than once. Throughout your journey you may only cross the equator a total of nine times: four by land, five by sea. Sea routes are illustrated by arrows which indicate your optional destinations.

Solution on page 85.

48

MATCH WITS #2

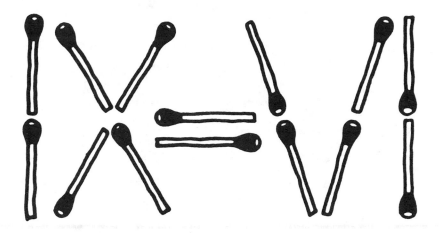

At present we see an equation that incorrectly tells us that the Roman numeral nine is equal to the Roman numeral six. Can you add three additional matches to this equation to make both sides equal?

Solution on page 87.

Clue to puzzle 39: Ruth and Gehrig wore the lowest numbers.

6 SHOOTER

Travel through this maze connecting each of the six spots with one continuous meandering line. No passageway or intersection may be used more than once. Your starting and finishing points are located in the dead-end passages.

Solution on page 88.

BOMBS AWEIGH

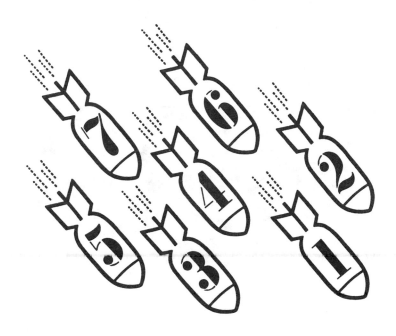

Five of the bombs in this puzzle are fully armed. Two of the bombs are unarmed and weigh half that of the armed bombs. From the following six groups of three bombs it is known that each threesome contains one unarmed bomb. Your task is to determine which two bombs are the lightweights.

1) 1, 2, 3   4) 4, 5, 6
2) 2, 3, 4   5) 5, 6, 7
3) 3, 4, 5   6) 6, 7, 1

Solution on page 91.

Three's a Crowd

333

One way of making three threes total eleven is to combine two threes making thirty-three and then dividing by the final three to give the desired result of eleven. Can you find another way to make this threesome produce eleven?

Solution on page 93.

Clue to puzzle **40**: *Begin by positioning* O-N-E *on the wheel.*

7 Letters

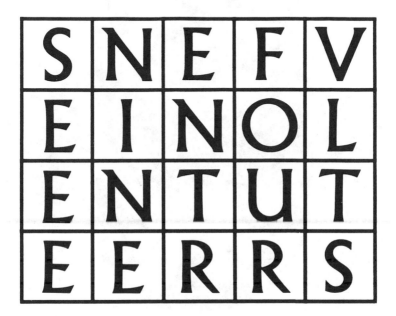

S	N	E	F	V
E	I	N	O	L
E	N	T	U	T
E	E	R	R	S

Cross out seven letters to reveal two numbers.

Solution on page 83.

Clue to puzzle **41**: *DAD = 505:*

50
PAPER MOONS

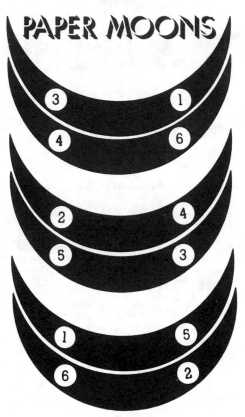

Currently, six paper moons are arranged in such a manner that the two lefthand and two righthand circles from each pair total seven. It is your task to rearrange the six paper moons so that a new configuration is created in which six new pairs of two circles also total seven. Adjacent moons in the current configurations may not be adjacent in the new solution.

Solution on page 85.

(Need a clue? turn to page 57.)

The $1,000 Pyramid

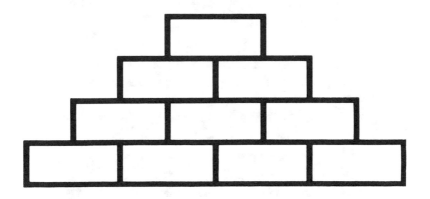

Using only the number eight, place ten money amounts in the ten blocks of this pyramid to total $1,000.

Solution on page 87.

(Need a clue? Turn to page 61.)

Clue to puzzle **42** *: Lowest score possible is forty-five points.*

Domino Switcheroo

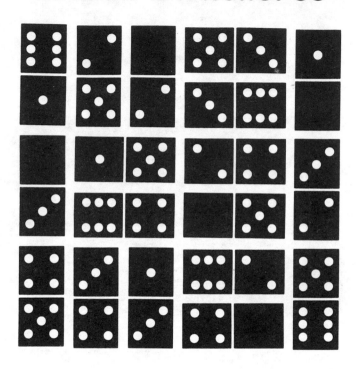

Switch the position of the fewest number of dominos in this puzzle to create a new six-by-six square in which no duplicate number of pips is repeated in any of the six columns or six rows. At present only the bottom row contains two identical four-pip squares.

Solution on page 89.

(Need a clue? Turn to page 62.)

EVEN STEVEN

Seven and eleven are both odd numbers. Your task is to make both numbers even without performing a single mathematical operation.

Solution on page 83.

Clue to puzzle **50**: *Arrange all six paper moons into a doughnut shape.*

3 RING CIRCUIT

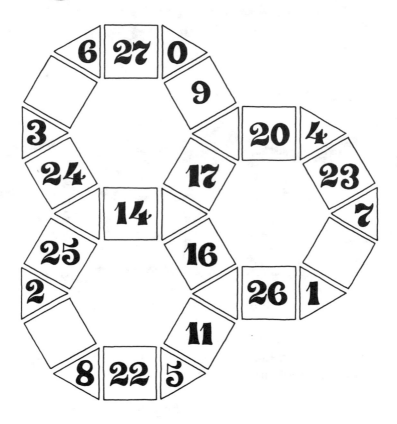

When this puzzle is completely solved, it will reveal
the numbers zero through twenty-seven. All you
have to do is position the remaining seven numbers
to assure that each of the three rings of twelve
numbers totals exactly the same number.

Solution on page 91.

Key Decision #2

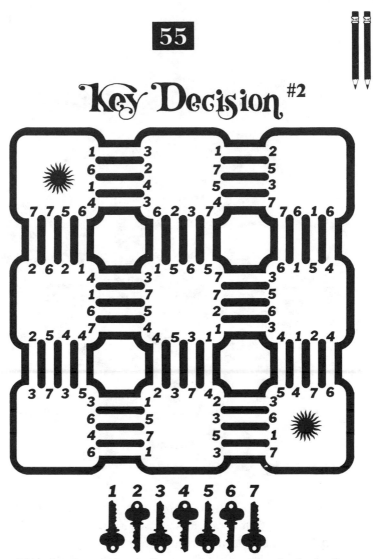

The numbered keys above correspond to the locked corridors in the puzzle. It is your challenge to select only three keys that will unlock the correct corridors and allow passage from one sunburst room to the other.

Solution on page 93.

Pathfinders

Four pathfinders have coordinated their efforts in such a way that each individual can travel from start to finish using a different route. Each route must pass through exactly six intersections, revealing the numbers one through six (in any order). No path or intersection may be utilized more than once per route. Can you trace the routes of these four pathfinders?

Solution on page 87.

PageMaster

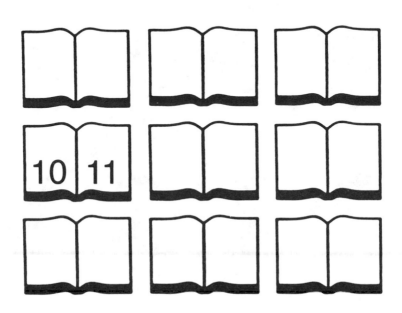

Position page numbers on the remaining eight books in such a way that a magic square is formed in which each horizontal, vertical, and diagonal row of three books (six pages) totals exactly 111. Note: Books are always folioed with the even-numbered page on the left.

Solution on page 83.

(Need a clue? Turn to page 65.)

Clue to puzzle **51**: *Think dollars and cents.*

MATCH WITS #3

2 2 2 1

Two minus two does not equal two minus one. Rearrange only two matches to make the equation equal on both sides. Illustrate your answer with the bottom set of numbers.

Solution on page 85.

(Need a clue? Turn to page 68.)

Clue to puzzle **52***: Only two dominos must be rearranged.*

59

FIREHOUSE SOLITARY

Position seven of the ten illustrated cards on the playing board as follows: 1) Identical suits may not appear in adjacent boxes. 2) Identical or consecutive face values may not appear in adjacent boxes. Ace is always low.

Solution on page 91.

PYRAMAZE

Place the remaining numbers, from one to twelve, in the vacant circles around the pyramid so that: 1) The ends of all six crisscrossing passages total the same number. 2) Each side of the pyramid adds up to a single number.

Solution on page 89.

(Need a clue? Turn to page 71.)

Win–Win Situation

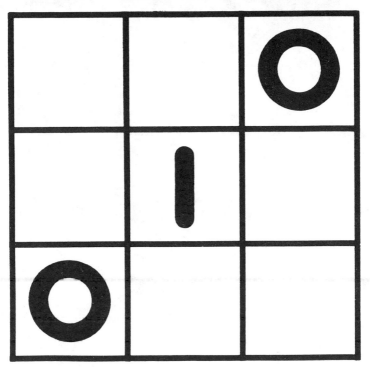

You'll create a win–win situation if you're clever enough to fill the remaining six squares with four numbers to complete this unique crossword-style number puzzle.

Solution on page 93.

(Need a clue? Turn to page 74.)

Clues to puzzle **57**: *The lowest page number is two; the highest is thirty-five.*

PHONY NUMBERS #2

Here is a coded word game in which the telephone is instrumental in converting numbers to letters. As seen on a touch-tone or dial phone, each of the numbers used in this puzzle can represent one of three different letters. It is your challenge to convert each line of numbers into a word which is related to its puzzle category. It takes one smooth operator to answer the call for each line of phony numbers in this collection of three categories.

Solution on page 83.

BREAKFAST FOODS

A•7287243
B•6286325
C•4727337848
D•72622537
E•2676352537

THINGS THAT ARE PULLED

A•82339
B•687253
C•8724567
D•83384
E•2277687

PANT-A-LOONY

A•25666377
B•267387697
C•386427337
D•56425377
E•752257

63

EWES YOUR HEAD

Nine shepherds herd nine flocks of consecutive numbers of sheep. Can you arrange these nine flock sizes in the nine ewes of this puzzle in such a way that each horizontal, vertical, and diagonal row of three ewes totals 1995?

Solution on page 85.

(Need a clue? Turn to page 75.)

Clue to puzzle **58**: *For starters, move the equals sign to the right.*

DOUBLE TROUBLE

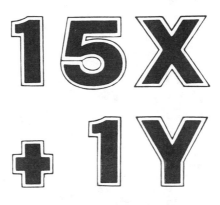

$$15X$$
$$+ 1Y$$
$$\overline{\qquad}$$
$$1Z$$

Here's a mathematical problem that has two correct and completely different solutions. You must solve for both solutions. In each case we're looking for fifteen of something (X) and one of something else (Y) that adds up to one of something else (Z). Example: If the problem were 3X + 2Y = 1Z, the answer could be 3 quarts + 2 pints = 1 gallon.

Solution on page 89.

(Need a clue? Turn to page 77.)

Cross Examination #2

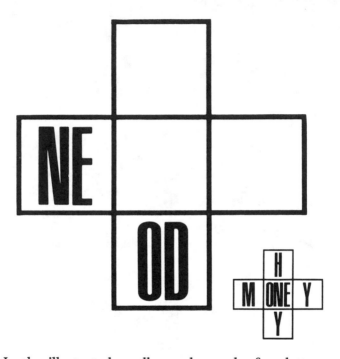

In the illustrated small sample puzzle, four letters (H, M, Y, Y) and one number (ONE) fill the five squares to create a mini-crossword number puzzle that spells "money" across and "honey" down. Your task is to solve the partially completed puzzle above by positioning one number in the center square and a total of six letters in the remaining two squares to reveal two words that fit the following clues:

Across: As easy as ABC.
Down: All washed up.

Solution on page 87.

Save Our Ships

S O S

Each of the ships in this puzzle has sent out a distress signal. Can you trace three paths from each ship that connect to each of the different letters of the S.O.S.? At no time may any of your lines cross one another or pass through ships.

Solution on page 93.

Clue to puzzle **60** : *Thirteen and twenty-six.*

Oval Office Frenzy

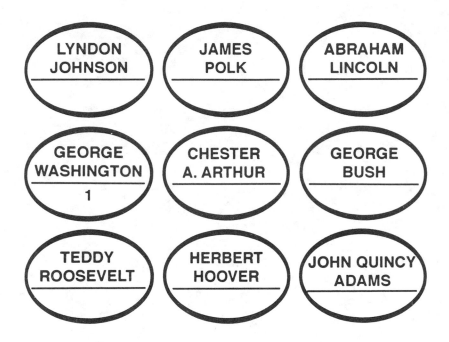

Positioned in nine oval offices are nine Presidents of the United States. These are the 1st, 6th, 11th, 16th, 21st, 26th, 31st, 36th, and 41st Presidents. Correctly number each President's term of office (as illustrated by the Washington oval office) and you'll create a magic square in which each horizontal, vertical, and diagonal row of three offices totals the same number.

Solution on page 91.

UNITED SQUARES
OF AMERICA

AL	WA	UT	CA	NY	VA	NJ
DE	FL	ND	WY	AK 1	PA	MD
SC	MA	IA	NE	ID	NV	TN
MS	KY	VT	WI	GA	KS	NM
TX	NC	ME	RI 49	AR	OK	OR
CO	MT	OH	WV	CT	IL	SD
MO	MN	AZ	LA	IN	NH	MI

Positioned above are the abbreviations of all forty-nine continental United States. Alaska, the largest state in area, is number one; Rhode Island, the smallest, is 49th. Rank the remaining continental states to create a magic square in which each horizontal, vertical, and diagonal row of seven squares totals 175. Even if you're not a geographic genius, a few educated guesses will manifest your destiny.

Solution on page 87.

One Eggstra

As illustrated, at present this carton holds exactly one dozen eggs. How is it possible to position thirteen eggs in this same carton without breaking or scrambling a single egg? Placing two eggs in any single compartment is not allowed.

Solution on page 85.

Clue to puzzle **61**: *The numbers you position must be in the form of words.*

FLUSTER 8

Travel through this maze connecting each of the seven spots with one continuous meandering line. No passageway or intersection may be used more than once. Your starting and finishing points are located in the dead-end passages.

Solution on page 93.

Clue to puzzle **63**: *The smallest flock is 661.*

Dice Decipher

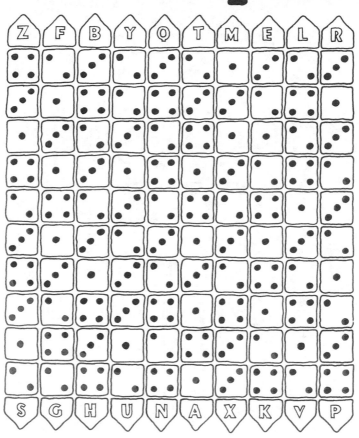

Using a four-number repetitive sequence (such as 2-4-1-3, 2-4-1-3, and so on), trace a path from any letter above to any letter below. You may move horizontally and vertically to any adjacent unused die.

Solution on page 85.

72

Round Numbers #2

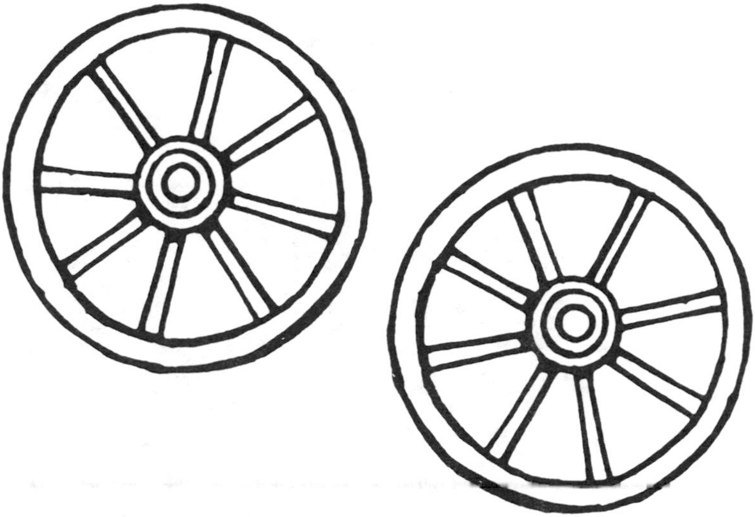

Position one letter in each of the eight between-spoke openings of these wagon wheels. Do this in such a way that you spell out four numbers (two in each wheel) which, taken together, total thirty-one. The numbers in this puzzle must all be written in a clockwise manner, but just as in traditional cross-word puzzles, individual letters may be shared. Example: Two and one could be written: TWONE.

Solution on page 87.

Clue to puzzle 64 *: In both solutions you must deal with "change."*

Trace Track

The numbers in this puzzle show the current position of four cars on this crisscrossing race track. As the three outer turnabout panels are currently arranged, only car 1 can cross the finish line. Rearrange three of the four turnabout panels around the center section of track to construct a single unending track that utilizes all road surfaces and will allow all cars to finish in the order 1, 2, 3, 4. Cars may not pass one another on this final lap.

Solution on page 91.

74

NUMERIC SHELVES

Rearrange the sixteen numbers in this puzzle to allow the two horizontal and two vertical rows of five squares to total the same number. There are twelve solvable totals. Your tasks are to construct the highest possible and lowest possible totals.

Solution on page 89.

MATCH WITS #4

Move two matches to make this equation equal.

Solution on page 93.

TEN NUMBERS

One of the eleven boxes above has already been filled. Fill the remaining ten boxes with ten numbers. If this is done correctly, the arrowed path will trace the final solution, which is smaller than Pi (3.141592 . . .) yet one larger than a number impossible to illustrate with Roman numerals.

Solution on page 89.

Lucky Lady

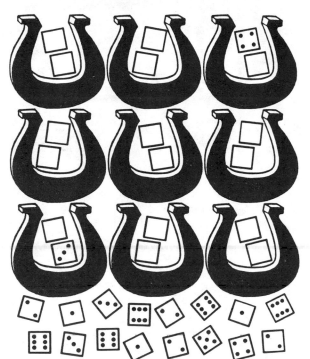

Nine pairs of dice are positioned in nine horseshoes in this puzzle. The pips are missing from all but two dice. From the illustrated sixteen dice you must add the pips to the blank dice to satisfy the following conditions: 1) Each horseshoe must total a different number. 2) Each horizontal, vertical, and diagonal row of three horseshoes must total twenty-one. 3) Doubles may not appear in any horseshoe.

Solution on page 91.

Solutions

1 With the maze upside down, the task becomes elementary.

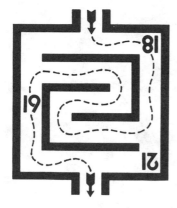

8

$6 \times 6 =$ 9 boards
$4 \times 4 =$ 25 boards
$2 \times 2 =$ <u>49 boards</u>
          83 total

15

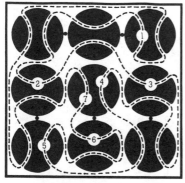

22 Each sequenced number represents the number of dots in progressively larger and proportional houses of dots whose width is always equal to its own height. The missing number is 127, a house of dots whose width and height measure thirteen dots.

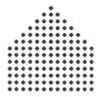

29

CHILDHOOD GAMES
A) hopscotch
B) jacks
C) marbles
D) leapfrog
E) tag

THINGS YOU OBSERVE
A) sabbath
B) laws
C) holidays
D) stars
E) customs

ON AN AIRPLANE
A) baggage
B) movie
C) pilot
D) stewardess
E) earphones

36

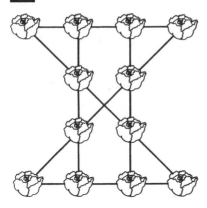

43 Eliminate W, K, and E. Substitute the Roman numerals V, X, and L.

```
V          5
I          1
C        100
X         10
L         50
D        500
───      ───
666      666
```

49

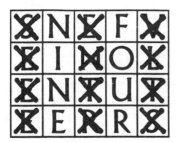

53 Remove "S" from seven, and "E" and "L" from eleven.

57 Reflection image also correct.

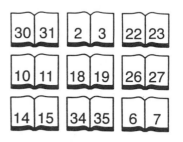

62

BREAKFAST FOODS
A) sausage
B) oatmeal
C) grapefruit
D) pancakes
E) cornflakes

THINGS THAT ARE PULLED
A) taffy
B) muscle
C) trailor
D) teeth
E) carrots

PANT-A-LOONY
A) bloomers
B) corduroys
C) dungarees
D) knickers
E) slacks

2

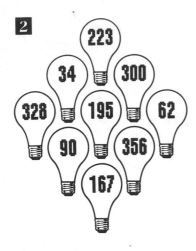

9 Reflection also correct.

18 The missing number is six. All of the numbers on this pyramid are "perfect." A perfect number is a number whose total divisions equal itself. Ex: 1, 2, 3 are all divisors of 6 and total six. 1, 2, 4, 7, 14 are all divisors of 28 and total 28. There are only 6 perfect numbers between 1 and 3,000,000.

23 Both puzzles are solved by using the face of a clock:
1) Starting at one, travel in a clockwise direction, counting every fifth number.
2) Starting at one, travel in a counterclockwise direction, moving first one number, then two numbers, then three, four, and five.

The use of the 12-hour division and the modern clock face did not exist in ancient Greece. The mechanical 12-hour clock was invented in the 1300s.

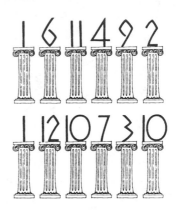

31

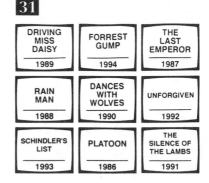

37

63 Reflections and rotations also correct.

44 From the dark star, proceed to 7, 3, 12, 6, 10, 2, 5, 8, 1, 9, 11, 4, white star. Reverse order also correct.

69

50

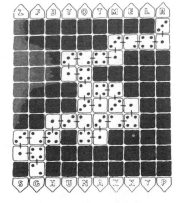

58 Two minus two halves equals one.

71

3

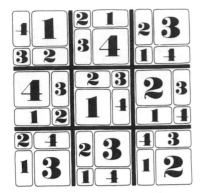

24

$$11$$
$$1.1$$
$$\overline{12.1}$$

10

30

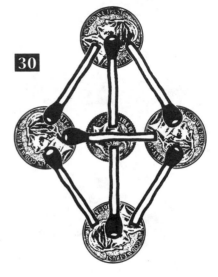

17

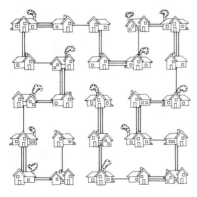

38

Begin at 6. End at 6. Score 66.

86

45 SIX equals VI.

51

56

A) 2, 3, 6, 4, 5, 1
B) 5, 6, 2, 1, 4, 3
C) 5, 6, 2, 3, 4, 1
D) 5, 6, 3, 4, 2, 1

65 NETWORK/DRIFTWOOD

68 Hawaii ranks 47th if you count all 50 states.

AL	WA	UT	CA	NY	VA	NJ
28	20	12	3	30	36	46
DE	FL	ND	WY	AK	PA	MD
48	26	17	9	1	32	42
SC	MA	IA	NE	ID	NV	TN
40	45	23	15	11	7	34
MS	KY	VT	WI	GA	KS	NM
31	37	43	25	21	13	5
TX	NC	ME	RI	AR	OK	OR
2	29	39	49	27	19	10
CO	MT	OH	WV	CT	IL	SD
8	4	35	41	47	24	16
MO	MN	AZ	LA	IN	NH	MI
18	14	6	33	38	44	22

72 Reflections and rotations also correct.

THREE
EIGHT
NINE
+ ELEVEN
THIRTY-ONE

4

1) 533 years 4 months
2) 333 years 4 months
3) 133 years 4 months

11

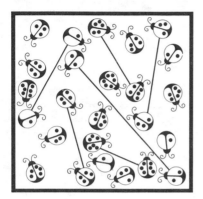

16 From Roman numeral eleven, illustrated (XI), remove the three matches below the dotted line to reveal Roman numeral six (VI).

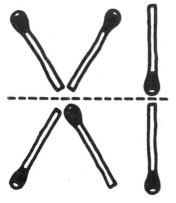

25

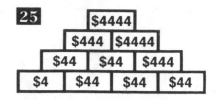

32 The rack is correct as is. Each diamond totals exactly twenty-one. Simply spin the six and nine balls 180 degrees to reveal their correct orientations.

39 In home run order:
Top: 7, 3, 8, and 4;
Middle: 5, 3, 8, and 6;
Bottom: 5, 7, 4, and 6.

3 Ruth
4 Gehrig
5 DiMaggio
6 Boyer
7 Mantle
8 Berra

46

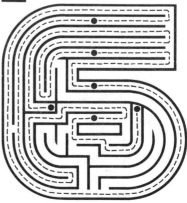

52 Switch the one/zero domino with the four/zero domino.

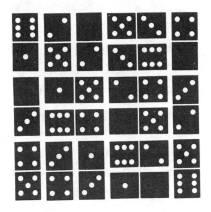

60

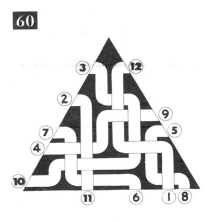

64

15 pennies	15 nickels
+ 1 dime	+ 1 quarter
1 quarter	1 dollar

74 Many variations exist for both solutions.

The lowest is 37.

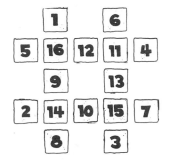

The highest is 48.

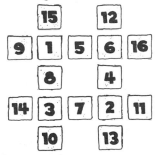

76 The concept of zero cannot be illustrated with Roman numerals.

The path reveals "number one."

89

5

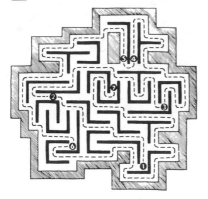

26

12

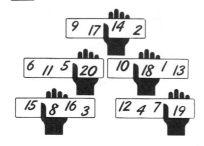

33 ANTENNA/PATENTS

19

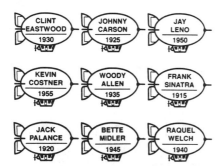

40 Reflections and rotations also correct.

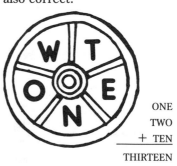

ONE
TWO
+ TEN
⎯⎯⎯⎯
THIRTEEN

47 Numerically the lightweights must be separated by two armed bombs. Since 1, 2, and 7 must be armed, the unarmed bombs must be 3 and 6.

67

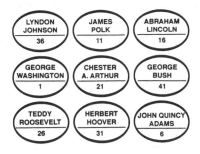

54 One of several possible solutions.

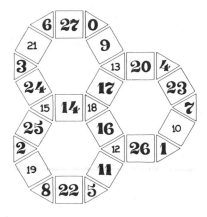

73

59 One of several variations.

77

6 It's easy once you realize that the two fathers and two sons total only three people: a grandfather, a son, and a grandson.

28

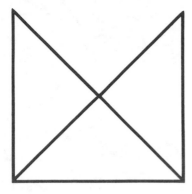

34 SUM, COMPUTE, FIGURE, CALCULATE, TOTAL, QUANTITY.

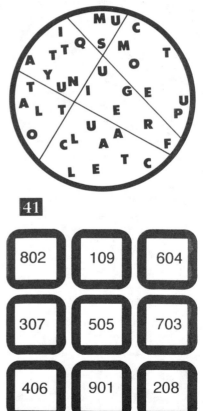

13 Numbers 9 and 25 may be reversed.

16	81	1	4
1	102		25
49			9
36	1	1	64

41

802	109	604
307	505	703
406	901	208

20

1, 3, 6, 2, 8, 4, 7, 9, 5, 1
or
1, 7, 4, 2, 8, 3, 6, 9, 5, 1

48 Combine the smallest and largest three to create the illustrated number eight. Now $8 + 3 = 11$.

55 Keys needed: 1, 3, 5.

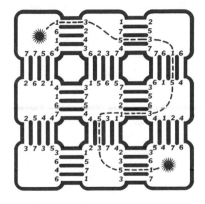

61

66 Variations of this solution exist, but in each case one of the lines must pass through the letter "O", otherwise this puzzle is impossible to solve.

70

75 This Roman numeral equation reads:
$100 = 10 \times 10$

7

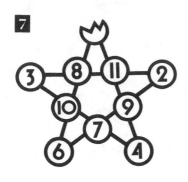

27

14

35 Rotations also correct.

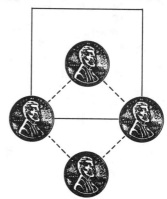

21 Keys needed: 2, 3, 4.

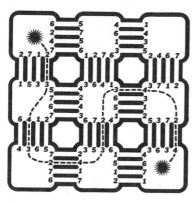

42

94

About the Author

If the world's greatest magician was Harry Houdini, and the world's greatest detective was Sherlock Holmes, then surely the world's greatest puzzle and game master is Steve Ryan, recognized as the most prolific creator of puzzles in the world, with more than 11,000 brain-busting bafflers to his credit.

This virtuoso of vexation has been inventing games and puzzles since childhood. He eventually found a market for his creations through Copley News Service, where his Puzzles & Posers and Zig-Zag features have appeared for more than twenty years and currently challenge readers in more than 150 newspapers across the United States and Canada.

Ryan's creative genius also catapulted him into television, where he co-created and developed the TV game show "Blockbusters" for television's most pretigious game-show packager, Mark Goodson. Ryan has also written for "Password Plus," "Trivia Trap," "Body Language," and "Catch Phrase," and created all the rebus puzzles for TV's "Classic Concentration." Currently, Ryan heads the development of new games for the Goodson Games lottery division with such creations as Beach Ball, Force Field, Splashdown, and Vortex for the lottery game shows in Florida, Illinois, Massachusetts, and Hungary.

Ryan is the author of more than a dozen popular books, including *Test Your Math IQ, Test Your Word Play IQ, Test Your Puzzle IQ, Pencil Puzzlers, Challenging Pencil Puzzlers,* and *Classic Concentration,* and co-author of the original and second edition of *The Encyclopedia of TV Game Shows,* the most comprehensive book of its kind. His puzzles have also appeared in *Games* magazine, and *Games & Puzzles* magazine in the United Kingdom. Worldwide, his puzzle books have been translated into Dutch, French, Indonesian, and Spanish, with other faraway lands soon to experience Ryan's puzzling world.

Many predicted Ryan's gifts in art, design, and mathematics would lead to architecture. But as usual, Ryan had a surprise twist in store: he built a mental gymnastics empire instead.

Nothing puzzling about that.

Puzzle Index

Puzzle [number] and page key: puzzle, *clue*, **solution**.